Contents

KU-750-553

CHAPTER 1

Ha ha, what's it all about?

Here's a question for you: Which came first, language or laughter?

If you guessed laughter, you'd be right. That's totally logical if you think about it. Most babies begin to laugh out loud at around 3 or 4 months old. Some take longer, but whenever it first happens, infants are chuckling long before they utter their earliest words.

Laughter is innate. In other words, it's a built-in ability. No one had to show you how to do it. One day you just burst out in spontaneous baby giggles, and you've been laughing without lessons ever since.

"People throughout history have laughed in pretty much the same way, which is a very curious business because we don't consciously decide to do it."

Dr Robert Provine,
neurobiologist

Humans laugh a lot. According to scientific studies, people laugh about seven times for every 10 minutes of talking together.

Now think about language, a learned skill. Even if you were a child genius, it took you a while to start talking. And with about 7,100 different languages in the world, communication between those who don't speak the same languages can be a real challenge. But you can share a laugh with anyone, even if you don't understand a single word they say.

What is laughter really all about? What's the psychological significance of it? Why do people tend to feel good about each other when they get caught in a chuckle-fest? And what's going on in your brain and your body when you start laughing your head off?

Researchers of all kinds have been working overtime to answer these questions. The things they've discovered might surprise you!

CHAPTER 2

Laughter:
helping social survival

WHEN YOU LAUGH, a lot happens in your body. This is one area in which the science is well understood. First, your face shows your emotion. You might scrunch your eyebrows or raise them. Your cheek and eye muscles go into a series of contractions. This is the "surprise response" kicking in, with as many as 15 facial muscles getting involved.

Next you begin breathing more quickly and your heart rate increases. Your diaphragm breaks into repeated, rhythmic muscle spasms that squeeze air out of your lungs. The noise that results sounds like a string of common vowel sounds, often something like "ha ha ha ha", "hee hee hee" or "ho ho" – the rising and falling sounds of laughter.

If you laugh really hard, your face may turn red and your tear ducts might overflow. You might look like a fish as you gasp for air, your mouth opening and closing. That's because the larynx partially closes and your air intake becomes irregular. Sometimes the muscles in other parts of your body go through changes too. Bottom line: Laughter is an expression of feeling that gives the body a real workout!

No matter what your laugh sounds like – whether it comes out as squeaking, hooting, snorting or barely any sound at all – it sends an emotional message, just as the cries and roars of some animals do. It has a definite social purpose.

The vowel sounds of laughter don't intermingle. In other words, when you're laughing you might make a ha-ha-ha sound or a ho-ho-ho sound, but it will never sound like ha-ho-ha-ho!

Laughing to survive

Many researchers believe the evolution of laughter, language and the brain itself occurred alongside the evolution of civilization. Thousands of years ago, human communities were few and far between. But as civilizations developed, populations grew larger and closer together. Living in large societies wasn't easy. The human brain needed to improve rapidly to deal with increasingly complex situations. Handling the demands of so many neighbours became a matter of survival.

Spontaneous laughter was an early part of the success package. It gave a sense of belonging. It reduced stress and helped humans get along better with the crowd. The ability to laugh was literally a way to stay alive.

The ability to laugh was literally a way to stay alive.

For one thing, laughter is usually a sign that everything is okay. It builds trust by sending the message that someone isn't a threat. Laughing with others is a clear way of saying we're all part of the same friendly group, sharing the same perspective on things. In other words, we're safe!

That's powerful non-verbal communication. It has worked well through the ages because one of the most important functions of laughter was, and still is, building social bonds. The minute you say something funny and get a laugh in response, you know you've got someone on your side. And if one of those people sharing the laughs happens to be somebody you're scared of, good news! Joint laughter might very well mean the threat isn't as real as you thought.

Animal kingdom giggles

Think of all the running, chasing and wrestling you did as a child – or maybe still do. That's a lot of playful fun. For every juvenile mammal on the planet, human or otherwise, play is an important part of learning and growing up.

During the best play times, you probably laughed your head off, and that's where things get strange. Most animals can't belly laugh. Science has identified only two other laughing mammals so far, and they couldn't be more different. They are apes and – surprisingly – rats.

Some researchers say the laughter-like vocalizations of these animals come from the more primitive part of the brain. It's the same part responsible for other animal vocalizations, such as roaring. In both rats and apes, giggles are triggered by play, mainly playful tickling.

In 2009, Dr Marina Davila-Ross, a psychologist, experimented with laughter in apes. Her goal was to trace the evolution of laughter and other types of vocalizations. She also wanted to find the laughter links connecting modern-day humans and apes to their ancient ancestors.

Davila-Ross conducted her study by travelling to zoos around the world. While she listened in and recorded sound, caretakers at each zoo tickled all kinds of apes, including bonobos, chimpanzees, gorillas and orangutans. The apes giggled lots! The sounds these animals made showed Davila-Ross that laughter is a cross-species phenomenon. In other words, when we talk about laughter in apes, we are not just using an anthropomorphic term to describe behaviour that is like laughter. The apes really are laughing.

Davila-Ross discovered that humans and apes probably get their ability to laugh from one common primate ancestor. She stated that humans must have started laughing at least 10 to 16 million years ago and very possibly long before.

"The caretakers play with the apes all the time, and tickling is a very important part of that. There are certain body parts that are more ticklish than others, depending on the individual. Some were tickled on their necks or armpits, while others offered their feet to be tickled."

Dr Marina Davila-Ross, psychologist

Rat laughs

Human beings don't share many genetic links with rats. But these little creatures love tickles, too. Check out the studies done by neuroscientist Jaak Panksepp. He took animal emotions seriously when most scientists thought only humans were capable of feeling.

Panksepp studied lab rats in the 1990s and found that tickling by hand really set them off. In fact, they enjoyed it so much that they chased after the tickler's hand, hoping for more play time. However, the high-pitched squeaks and chirps of rat laughter are impossible for the human ear to pick up. So Panksepp, sometimes referred to as "the rat tickler", used ultrasonic equipment to listen. What he heard was a sound he thought of as pure joy. The rats also chirped in delight when they came into new environments or when they expected some kind of reward.

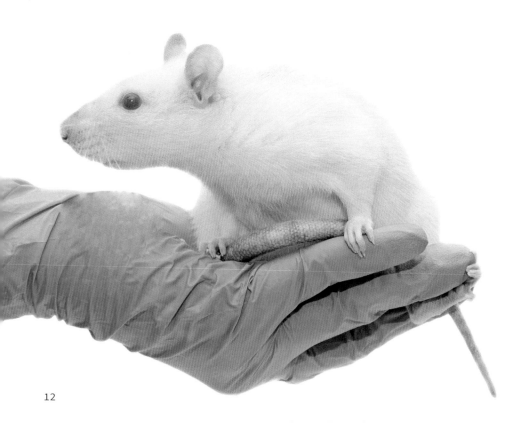

Panksepp's work with rats told him a lot about laughter in general. It also led to the development of a new antidepressant medication and other advancements in treating depression. To put it plainly, his research into laughing rats was no joke!

TICKLED PINK

You're messing around with your brother when he starts tickling you so hard you can barely stand it. You squirm, giggle, try to push him off, laugh out loud. Finally he lets you go. Your face is flushed. You're breathing hard. And you're extremely relieved to be out of his clutches. Even though you may laugh out loud when it's happening, prolonged tickling often doesn't feel that good to humans. So why do you laugh?

Take it back to the brain. While tickling may be OK for a short time and feel like enjoyable bonding, tickling stimulates nerve fibres that trigger pain. When you laugh while being tickled, two areas of the brain become active. These are the Rolandic operculum (which controls facial, vocal and emotional reactions) and the hypothalamus. Why does the hypothalamus react when you're being tortured by tickling? Neuroscientists say it's because the hypothalamus generates that age-old impulse to flee danger.

Have you ever tried to tickle yourself? Odds are that it didn't work. Why? Blame it on your cerebellum. Researchers believe that this part of your brain, located at the base of your skull, is responsible for predicting how certain movements will feel. Knowing the sensations that tickling causes, your cerebellum just doesn't let the other areas of the brain respond when you try to tickle yourself.

Try this!

Put your ticklish brain to the test. Take off your left shoe and sock and cross your left leg over your right thigh. Then ask a friend to sit next to you on the right. Now totally relax and let your friend take your right hand and extend your index finger forwards. Keep your hand completely relaxed while your friend moves your finger, tickling the arch of your bare foot. Does your brain believe someone else is tickling you, or will you fail at fooling it?

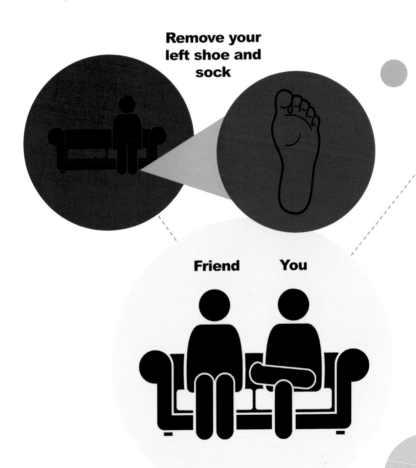

Remove your left shoe and sock

Friend   **You**

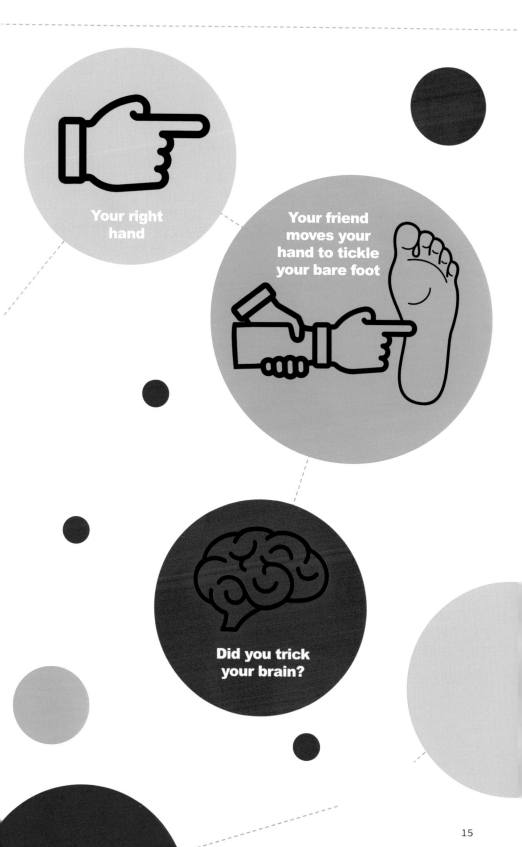

Your right hand

Your friend moves your hand to tickle your bare foot

Did you trick your brain?

15

CHAPTER 3

The feel-good phenomenon

WE LAUGH AND IT'S not a big deal. But for scientists in the field of gelotology, it's a different story. Gelotologists study what happens to a person when laughter occurs. What are the effects of humour on the mind and body? What happens when someone is under the influence of laughter? Research has revealed that the laughter "circuit" runs through many parts of the brain, and we get our laughs through a complicated interaction among these parts.

The word *gelotology* comes from the Greek word *gelos*, meaning "laughter". In ancient Greek mythology, Gelos was the god of laughter.

Your brain on laughter

Somebody says something funny, and you burst out in a short guffaw. Even in just those few seconds, an incredible amount of information processing goes on inside your skull. It all starts with the largest and outermost part of the brain. It's that big wrinkly mass known as the cerebral cortex.

Each side of the cerebral cortex has four lobes that control our higher thought processes: the frontal, parietal, occipital and temporal lobes. Two of the most important higher thought processes are decision making and the ability to speak. The cortex also reviews information that comes through the five senses.

Laughter parts of the brain

FRONTAL LOBE

THALAMUS

OCCIPITAL LOBE

HYPOTHALAMUS

AMYGDALA

HIPPOCAMPUS

A lot of action goes on in various areas of the cortex when we laugh, but other parts are involved as well. Take a look!

- **FRONTAL LOBE:** Partially responsible for sorting out social-emotional responses

  A major factor in laughter, the frontal lobe lets us know if something is funny or not. Without its help, you might not be able to tell whether or not to laugh.

- **OCCIPITAL LOBE:** Processes sensory input and plays a key role in making laughter happen

  This lobe is vision headquarters. It processes signals from your eyes and helps you to decode those signals – assigning meaning to what you see. When it comes to laughter, the occipital lobe helps you understand facial expressions, gestures and other aspects of physical humour.

- **LIMBIC SYSTEM:** Responsible for the development and expression of emotions, especially the basics of love, fear and pleasure

  This group of small structures is located deep in the brain, beneath the temporal lobe, and includes the amygdala, the hippocampus, the thalamus and the hypothalamus. It is important in the formation of memories and the experience of pleasure, including – that's right – laughter.

Another way of grasping how laughter happens is to consider the brain's left and right hemispheres. When it comes to humour, or jokes, the left hemisphere takes on the first task, analyzing the words and structure of the joke. Then the right hemisphere performs an intellectual analysis, finding the meaning that makes it possible for us to get the joke. The right hemisphere is especially involved when it comes to more sophisticated humour.

Wired for laughter

The electroencephalograph, or EEG, measures electrical activity in the brain and is a basic tool for some gelotologists. One laughter study looked at EEG patterns and found that the brain reacts within four-tenths of a second when presented with something funny. In the lab, just the introduction of something humorous caused an electrical wave to move instantaneously through the cerebral cortex.

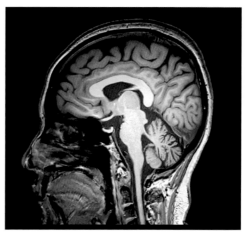

Other studies of the brain have used functional magnetic resonance imaging (fMRI) to learn about laughter. In one of these, neuroscientist Dr Sophie Scott had volunteers listen to a series of different sounds, both positive, such as triumphant shouts and laughter, and negative, such as retching and screaming. As the subjects listened, Scott's team watched their brain activity with an fMRI scanner. In every case, the sounds triggered a response in the premotor cortical region. This is the part of the brain that prepares our facial muscles to move in ways that correspond to sounds we hear.

The overall response was greater in reaction to the positive sounds. Most of the subjects smiled when they heard laughter or other positive sounds. But when they heard the sound of vomiting, for example, they showed no equivalent response, such as gagging.

For Scott, the interpretation was obvious: Positive sounds are more contagious than negative sounds. Think about it. If someone around you starts laughing, you're likely to find yourself smiling involuntarily – even if you don't know what's funny. It's the same principle. We humans gravitate to what makes us feel good and, Scott believes, have a built-in desire to avoid negative sounds and feelings.

Laughter as a social signal

Laughter is a language we all speak. And we know it serves in the valuable task of human social bonding. But the ha-ha's aren't just about people thinking we're funny. In fact, it's not so much about that at all. Getting the giggles is mainly an automatic clue that lets others know how we're feeling.

Dr Panksepp, the rat tickler, theorized that laughing in rats showed emotional health. Panksepp observed that young rats were often drawn to the rats that laughed more often. This suggested that laughter helped the rats bond socially more easily with their friends. Could the same be said of humans? It could.

Social laughter is an area of fascinating research. One big thing scientists have found is that manufacturing laughter in a lab setting doesn't work so well. One behavioural neurobiologist, Dr Robert R Provine, asked people to sit alone and watch comedy videos. But no one laughed uproariously. They barely laughed at all. In the end, Provine found that social laughter, or laughing with others, is 30 times more common than solitary laughter. That's a lot!

Next, Provine went out into the field. Hoping for better insights into social laughter, he spent 10 years observing people. He and a few undergraduate assistants eavesdropped on laughing people in classrooms, parties and shopping centres.

The researchers tracked more than 2,000 incidents of people laughing together. They found that, most of the time, conversational laughter is like punctuation. It usually happens at the end of sentences or comments, not before them or in the midst of speaking. This is true even of people who use sign language, although they can laugh and sign at the same time.

Incredibly, during all this laughing, actual humorous content was rarely involved. People laughed at things purposely meant to be funny, such as stories or jokes, less than 20 per cent of the time. Much more mundane comments brought on most of the chuckles. Provine determined that a sense of friendly togetherness, the upbeat tone of the exchanges, and a mutual playfulness caused most of the laughter. Keep a close watch on your own social circles and you may find the same thing.

Obviously, a good laugh makes us feel great. Another study proved this by performing two positron emission tomography (PET) scans on volunteers. This type of scan uses a radioactive chemical to see activity in the brain and other organs. One scan was done after the subjects had engaged in a 30-minute "social laughter session". The other was done after they had spent 30 minutes alone in a room. Not surprisingly, the laugh-fests triggered a greater release of the brain's feel-good chemicals than sitting around alone did. And those chemicals came from the parts of the brain associated with arousal, reward and a few other human impulses.

You've probably guessed this already, but gelotology has proven that genuine laughter is triggered by human relationships, not humour in and of itself.

. . . genuine laughter is triggered by human relationships . . .

LAUGH NOW

LAUGHING ON CUE

On 9 September 1950, a groundbreaking event occurred on TV. People tuning in to *The Hank McCune Show,* an early US sitcom, heard laughter from an unseen audience every time there was a moment of humour. But what the viewers heard wasn't a studio audience watching the show live. It was the first-ever laugh track, a burst of group laughter prerecorded and added to the funny bits.

Back then television was a new frontier. Trends and traditions were only just beginning. "Canned laughter" was a big idea that has never quite gone away – probably because it works. Because people are more likely to laugh with other people, laugh tracks make it easier for people alone at home to go along with a chuckle. When shows started using laugh tracks, many actors, critics and producers objected fiercely. Some just didn't like the fakery of it. Others felt it was an insult to viewers, as if they were too stupid to know when something was funny.

Today laugh tracks are much rarer. Most new sitcoms are filmed in front of live studio audiences or don't include laughter prompts at all. When shows do use canned laughs, they aren't the boisterous, uncontrolled howling of the early tracks. Yet, when the tracks are done well, the shows they are used on tend to have higher ratings and keep audiences watching for longer.

CHAPTER 4

LOL:
different jokes
for different folks

L OL. THESE THREE LETTERS JOINED together have become an international symbol that almost any digitally aware person can translate without thinking twice. Laughing out loud. We love to do it. We love to make it happen in others. It's a great group activity. But what actually makes you laugh? Brain chemistry aside, you might come up with multiple answers. Jokes. Humorous situations. Funny stories. Social cues. Tickling. Your friend's bad impersonations. Laughing gas.

Although LOL is a standard acronym in much of the world, how is it expressed in different languages? Here are a few LOL equivalents.

- Japan: wwww (The more *W*s you add, the funnier you think something is.)
- Thailand: 55555 (The word *five* is pronounced "ha" in Thai, so 5555 = hahahaha.)
- French: MDR (It's short for *mort de rire,* or "dying of laughter".)
- Spanish: jajaja (In Spanish, the *J* sound is pronounced "ha".)
- Greek: xaxa ("Ha ha" in Greek.)
- Korean: kkkk (Yet another "ha ha" sound.)
- Hebrew: xà xà xà (And another way of spelling "ha ha".)

Any of these could do it. But when it comes to funny stuff, getting a good laugh is not the same thing as humour. In earlier times, many people tried to sort this out. Philosophers such as the ancient Greeks Plato and Aristotle, as well as later thinkers such as Immanuel Kant and Sigmund Freud, tried to understand laughter by theorizing about humour. They didn't get anywhere. Humour and laughter have a cause-and-effect relationship. Humour is the cause. Laughter is the mind and body's spontaneous reaction to that humour.

Comedians work hard to come up with a formula for getting laughs. Some rely on one or two tried-and-tested methods. But there are plenty of theories on what makes us crack up with laughter. The three main theories point to relief, superiority and incongruity as things that get us giggling.

"Plato and Aristotle ... wanted to learn about laughter to control it... They were aware that laughter could lead to disrespect for authority and the overthrow of the state."

Dr Robert Provine,
neurobiologist

Plato

The three theories behind humour

RELIEF THEORY

People often experience rising emotional tension as they wait for an outcome, such as the punchline to a joke. Filmmakers use this technique all the time. Think of a fast-paced action film or thriller. You're sitting there, biting your nails, and just as your anxiety peaks, one of the characters makes a funny comment. This unexpected moment breaks the tension and gives you a much-needed emotional release. Then the tension starts mounting again . . .

SUPERIORITY THEORY

If you've ever heard the phrase, "I'm not laughing with you, I'm laughing at you," you'll recognize this one. It's the idea that people will laugh at things that make them feel as if they are better than others. In comedy, these jokes focus on someone's inferiority – often that of the person telling them. People can listen to gags about someone else's faults, foolish actions or misfortune and feel superior. Because they are emotionally detached from the bad situation, laughter results.

INCONGRUITY THEORY

This may be the most complex hypothesis about how humour makes people laugh. Basically, we get our sense of reality from the patterns stored in our brains. The mind has to sort through a constant, massive stream of incoming information. To make sense of it all, the mind looks for familiar patterns and filters out the rest. For example, most of us recognize familiar faces. The brain gives a lot of attention to anything similar to what has come before, especially if it's important input. If a stranger happens to look like someone who bullied you, your impulse might be to walk the other way. If they look like your best friend, you might be more willing to introduce yourself.

According to incongruity theory, laughter happens when a familiar pattern takes an unexpected turn. Your best friend posts a selfie of her face swapped with her dog's. Two things are put together that wouldn't normally go together at all. We experience the incongruity both mentally and emotionally, and that gives us a good chuckle. A good example of this is an old joke: A judge yells, "Order, order in the court!" and the defendant answers, "OK, I'll have cheese on toast, Your Honour." It's funny because of the incongruity between two meanings of the word *order*.

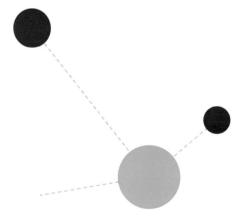

Group laughter

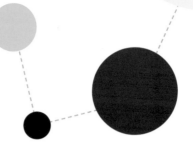

You're at the dinner table and you say something witty, maybe a sly comment about something that happened at school. Your siblings get a good laugh. But your parents? They roll their eyes or pay no attention at all. It all comes down to one thing. People differ a lot in what gives them the giggles. And you can usually break it down by groups. The main divisions are by age, gender, social status and cultural background, but there are others.

Age is one of the greatest factors in what people find funny. As a toddler you were focussed ot discovering the world. It was an exciting new place. The things that made you laugh were peek-a-boo, tickling, silly jokes and other simple but unexpected stuff.

As your sense of humour began to develop, it became a little subtler. But not too subtle! In primary school you probably started laughing about really silly or embarrassing things like bodily functions (and yeah, maybe "potty humour" is still funny even now). As a preteen or teen, now on the road to becoming independent, you're no doubt testing your boundaries. For example, you get a lot of laughs from things you know adults won't approve of – don't you?

Humour research has learned things about teens that probably wouldn't shock you. Teens like jokes about food, about challenging authority figures, and about any subject that adults consider off-limits. Scientists also say that because teen years are often a time of insecurity, funny stuff that fits with the superiority theory gets big laughs. Humour that cuts the everyday tension goes well, too.

"Laughter . . . does in the nervous system what a pressure-relief valve does in a steam boiler."

Dr John Morreall,
philosopher

As people become adults, their sense of humour broadens and becomes more complex. Adults are more likely to laugh with rather than at each other. That's because adults have a sharper awareness of the collective human experience – we all go through some of the same stuff, and we're all in this together. So a lot of what adults find funny stems from the embarrassments and ridiculousness of certain life situations.

No matter where we are in our life's journey, a lot of what we laugh at involves the stresses we're facing. If we're feeling a lot of tension about something and somebody cracks a joke about it, we might very well burst out in laughter – easing the tension, at least for the moment.

Gender and laughter

Are you a class clown? Do you love getting the giggles? Humans like to laugh, and we laugh a lot regardless of gender. In his studies, though, Provine found that gender may affect who you want to laugh with. People of all genders prefer romantic partners with a sense of humour. But, in studying laughter in interactions between men and women, he observed that women laugh much more in conversation than men do.

Provine found that, in conversations between men and women, the girls laughed a whopping 126 per cent more than the boys. Provine then studied 3,745 personal ads. He found that women seeking men in the ads mentioned "sense of humour" as a desirable trait 62 per cent more often than men seeking women did. Women mentioned their own sense of humour only half as often. Meanwhile, a higher percentage of men seeking women claimed being funny as one of their favourable qualities. But most of the men weren't looking specifically for women who would make them laugh. Provine suggested that women might be using laughter in conversation to help find romantic partners, and men respond by trying to inspire laughs.

Researchers still have more to learn about laughter and gender. It makes sense that people would want good laughing partners in a relationship. But gender is only one of several things that affect when and why we laugh. Provine discovered another thing in his research: Everyone in the study laughed more at men than they did at women. Why? The answer may involve social status and power.

Rungs of the ladder

Believe it or not, humour and laughter can reveal your social status. Let's say someone in your group makes a mistake that creates a funny incongruity and everybody laughs about it. In that moment the person you're laughing at is demeaned – their social status takes a temporary nose dive. Being made fun of is painful in more ways than one. It hurts emotionally. And if it happens enough, it can signal a long-term loss of status within the group.

Your place in the pecking order is also often indicated by when you laugh. Studies have shown that people who hear an unfunny joke will laugh less if they're a person in control in their world, such as a headteacher or a boss. When the same jokes were tested on people who had less authority – the boss's employees, for instance – they laughed a lot more if their leader did. Why is that?

Research has found that people in positions of authority, such as bosses, teachers, heads of families or religious leaders, laugh more than the people they direct. People with more power feel free to laugh at whatever they find funny – and to ignore what they don't. Why would someone who calls the shots feel the need to laugh at something unfunny? But when they think something is funny, even if it's silly or unkind, they laugh. They don't worry about losing social status by laughing at the wrong thing.

But studies show that those with less power are more likely to laugh at whatever the most powerful person laughs at. If your headteacher finds a joke funny and laughs, the teachers and staff will probably laugh too, even if they don't think the joke is worthy of laughter.

American philosopher John Morreall has given this a lot of thought. He is a member of the International Society for Humour Studies. He claims that controlling the laughter of a group is a power play. The leader of a group can use laughter to change the behaviour of others.

We've probably all done this at some point, whether we're the big cheese or lower on the social ladder. For example, if you feel nervous or embarrassed around your school's most notorious troublemaker, you might make a witty comment or find a reason to laugh when they're around. This could send the signal that you're not looking for a fight. If your troublesome classmate laughs with you, it's good news for you. It means there's enough trust – at least for the moment – to avoid conflict.

Even if a person doesn't know you, they might be able to tell where you stand in your social circle just by your style of laughter. In 2016, researchers brought together 48 men from the same college alumni and divided them into groups. Each group included two long-time members and two who had just joined.

When the scientists recorded each group joking around and teasing each other, they found interesting differences in how they laughed. Those who'd been part of the group for longer laughed louder, and the tones of their laughter varied more. It communicated dominance. The laughter of the newer members tended to be shorter, higher-pitched and more controlled.

"When you feel powerful, you feel relaxed," the head researcher claimed. When you feel relaxed and in control, you're less shy about your behaviour. This study only looked at male behaviour. The scientists noted they might find different laughing patterns in a study of women.

YOU CAN'T JUST FAKE IT

Next time you feel forced to laugh at something you don't find funny, think twice. In a recent study, volunteers listened to clips of both genuine and fake laughter. As they listened, the volunteers were able to pick out the fake laughter. In another study, fMRI scans revealed that hearing fake laughter triggers more action in the brain's medial prefrontal cortex, which is to do with problem solving. In other words, the listener is trying to work out why the person is faking it. When the laughter is the real thing, there's nothing to wonder about, and the only regions that fire up are the temporal lobe's auditory areas – the spot where sound is processed.

World wide wit

Culturally, what prompts laughter varies. That's to be expected. As humans formed individual and culturally diverse societies, our collective sense of humour diversified too. So what gets streams of laughter in one culture may not translate well at all in another. And yet, the prompts that make people laugh are pretty much the same everywhere. Studies have shown that humour based on incongruity theory gets laughs all around the world. So do techniques such as understatement, sarcasm, exaggeration, verbal irony and deception.

What's *your* favourite joke? Do you think someone from another country would find it funny? Maybe, maybe not. To learn what people from different cultures thought was funny, psychologist Dr Richard Wiseman created the LaughLab Project. He first asked people to submit jokes to the LaughLab. Then he asked them to rate five random jokes on how funny they were. It was a huge project, with more than 40,000 entries and more than 350,000 people participating from 70 countries. When the results were in, Wiseman broke down the votes according to country.

Americans and Canadians showed a strong preference for jokes that had a sense of superiority. People from the UK, Australia and Ireland preferred jokes that involved word play. People in Belgium, Denmark, France and some other European countries enjoyed jokes with incongruities. They also liked jokes that made fun of anxiety-producing experiences, including illness, death and marriage.

Many of the jokes relied on one of the theories of humour, of course. The favourite joke of Scottish voters was another perfect example of incongruity theory at work. It goes like this: "I want to die peacefully in my sleep like my grandfather did. Not screaming in terror like his passengers."

"When we laugh, how we laugh, what we laugh about, who makes us laugh, why we stop laughing, how we stop ourselves from laughing – all that is about control because laughter is literally the loss of control."

Dr Annette Goodheart,
psychologist

That's not funny!

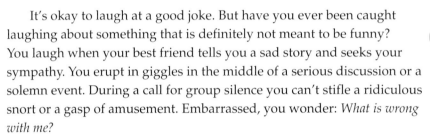

It's okay to laugh at a good joke. But have you ever been caught laughing about something that is definitely not meant to be funny? You laugh when your best friend tells you a sad story and seeks your sympathy. You erupt in giggles in the middle of a serious discussion or a solemn event. During a call for group silence you can't stifle a ridiculous snort or a gasp of amusement. Embarrassed, you wonder: *What is wrong with me?*

Nothing. Science has proven that this is perfectly natural. Researchers call it the inappropriate affect or, more simply, nervous laughter. In a tense or strained situation – or if you're just feeling awkward – the brain looks for an outlet to keep things cool. That outlet is often found in laughter.

Dr Steve Ellen, an Australian psychiatrist, believes inappropriate laughter is a psychological reaction. If we're anxious, he says, "our own body makes us start laughing to relieve the tension, even if we don't really want to [and] we'd prefer to be serious."

Stanley Milgram's so-called obedience experiments of 1961 seem to confirm this. In these famous studies, test subjects were given the role of "teachers" who punished wrong answers with electrical shocks. The "teachers" were not told that the "learners" were actors who were not really getting shocked. After giving a few shocks, some subjects quit. But many remained. And 14 of them broke out into uncontrollable laughter during the experiment. In interviews afterwards, these "teachers" said they felt embarrassed. They had not really enjoyed seeing someone suffer, but they couldn't help laughing. Stress, fear and discomfort made them laugh.

Inappropriate laughter is also incredibly contagious. Neuroscientist Dr Sophie Scott studied what makes people laugh. The thing most likely to get her test subjects giggling was video clips of people trying not to laugh in inappropriate situations. One particularly irresistible clip showed a news reader who had an uncontrollable laughing attack while trying to read the news on live TV. Just watching her attempts to hold back the laughs made Scott's test subjects laugh equally hard.

How many times have you tried to stifle your laughter, only to have the person next to you start howling too? And it spreads from there. The whole situation is so awful that you can't help laughing even harder. The added stress of recognizing just how *wrong* it is to be laughing only increases the urge to let it rip.

When the human brain detects laughter, certain neural circuits are triggered. This leads to more laughter, which in turn can lead to a very embarrassing situation. But next time you're hit by inappropriate laughter, breathe easy – if you can. It's a normal thing!

THE TANGANYIKA LAUGHTER EPIDEMIC

We can barely control a strong impulse to laugh. It's spontaneous and often catching. But sometimes that contagion can go too far. That was the case in 1962, in a small village in Tanganyika (today's Tanzania) in Africa. There, a bizarre laughter outbreak began in a school classroom. At the end of January that year, three girls began to giggle. They couldn't stop. Soon 95 students were laughing uncontrollably. By mid–March the unstoppable laughter had infected so many that the school had to close. But that just made things worse.

Giggle attacks began to hit others far and wide – and rapidly. Family members, neighbours and friends were bitten by the laughing bug too. The contagion soon spread to other schools and villages in central Africa. People laughed so hard they fainted. They had breathing troubles and stomach pains. They couldn't stop laughing.

The laughter eventually infected about 1,000 people. Reports vary, claiming the laughing fits lasted anywhere from six months to two and a half years. Over time, the uncontrollable urges to laugh faded away. That is one strange way to get out of school!

Get over it!

Think back to a time when laughter erupted – or threatened to erupt – at a really inappropriate moment. For some people, it happens in sad situations, such as a funeral. Scientists tell us a setting like that can cause anxiety as people start thinking about death, mortality or the loss of someone close. Laughter at moments such as these is common. But if you feel inappropriate laughter coming on, try one of these ways to squelch it.

• **BREATHE DEEP:** Close your eyes and focus on your breathing. Take many deep, slow breaths, which help reduce anxiety and may calm you down again. If you can breathe deeply for 90 seconds, your brain has the chance to regulate neurochemicals and bring the mental chemistry back to normal.

- **REDIRECT YOUR MIND:** Try to mentally list the names of everyone in your family. Think of a situation you experienced that wasn't funny at all. Focus your attention on a difficult maths problem or an upcoming piece of homework. Anything you can do to take your mind off the here and now should help.

- **PRETEND YOU'RE CRYING:** Tears can happen when you laugh really hard. And hard laughter can look and sound much like crying. So try to fake it till you make it. In a situation where laughter is really inappropriate, crying will probably seem more acceptable to those you're with.

- **BITE DOWN:** A little bit of pain might redirect your emotions. Pinch yourself hard. Try biting your lip or the insides of your cheeks for as long as you can stand it.

- **TRY THINKING "STOP":** But be careful. For some people, that word has the opposite effect, making matters worse.

CHAPTER 5

The dark side of laughter

LAUGHTER IS A GREAT STRESS RELIEVER. Collectively cracking up over something funny connects you and your friends and builds trust. Laughter sends good chemicals through your body to ease your pain. Plain and simple, laughing is just a lot of fun. Except when it's not.

As Dr Robert Provine says, "In our feel-good, be-happy society we always associate laughter with positive things, forgetting that laughter has a dark side. It's great laughing with friends . . . but it can be painful, even dangerous, if you're laughing *at* someone, or if they're laughing at you."

Teasing and bullying, which often involve laughing at others, are rampant in today's society. Even worse, both happen often on social media. It seems no one is safe from being laughed at or ridiculed, especially when it happens online. In the teen world, making fun of others has resulted in suicide attempts. Superiority-theory humour is one thing when it's all in fun. But taken to the real-life level of hurting someone else, laughter is a vicious power tool.

Left out

At some time or another, you've probably been on the outside when others were laughing – maybe at your expense. If so, you've been a victim of what researchers at Ohio State University in the USA call "exclusive laughter", or laughing *at* rather than *with* someone. In a study done there, subjects were asked to recount a time when they were the victims of exclusive laughter. The participants remembered the pain well. Two other groups were asked to recall either experiences of inclusive laughter or simply a typical Wednesday. When they rated their feelings in recalling the event, the participants who remembered being laughed at felt more ostracized. Their moods worsened, and they felt stronger impulses to be aggressive. Compared to the other two groups, those who were excluded also felt a greater amount of social pain and other negative responses.

These results are no surprise. Who wouldn't feel that way? But what might surprise you is that, for some people, just hearing others' laughter sparks an irrational fear. And that fear has a name: *gelotophobia.* Nobody likes being the butt of a joke, but gelotophobes take it to an extreme. Whenever they hear someone laughing, they believe that the laughter is malicious and directed at them. They're terrified just by the sound.

Hoping to come to the rescue, scientists from Switzerland, Africa, Canada, India, Russia and other countries are looking into the causes of gelotophobia. They know that people who suffer this condition often avoid being around others. Some experience dizzy spells or stress-related headaches. They may have high anxiety and depression. And many of them feel shame about their extreme fear, or phobia. So it might be good to take it easy on anyone who spends a lot of time alone. By teasing and laughing, you may be causing harm to that person.

Research into gelotophobia is relatively new – studies began in 2008 – and there's no medical treatment so far. Various types of therapy are being researched. The suspected causes of this condition may have to do with a traumatic experience in a child's early life, especially in school or at home. A young person who is ridiculed, laughed at, bullied, or not taken seriously might become a gelotophobe. Scientists are looking at a number of factors, including how children's personalities develop, what their social lives are like, and what kind of sense of humour they have themselves.

"Many people who are teased as children are terrified of laughter – their own as well as other people's. They were laughed at so much that they now react negatively to laughter as though it is always aimed at them."

Dr Annette Goodheart, psychologist

Warning signs

There's still a lot to learn about treating gelotophobia. But if you suspect it affects you or someone you know, the best choice is to get help from a psychologist or psychiatrist. Here are some symptoms that may point to gelotophobia.

Finding no fun in laughter and humour

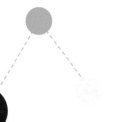

Lacking a sense of humour

Avoiding social interactions for fear of ridicule

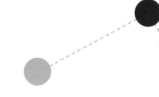

Lacking in joy and lively energy

Experiencing physical issues such as blushing or tension headaches

Researchers find less gelotophobia in Denmark than anywhere else in the world. That's because laughing at others is a major social no-no there. It's just not done.

Too much of a not-good thing

Laughter seldom causes physical problems, but it can be a sign of them. Pathological laughing or crying (PLC), as it's known, is laughter or crying that often isn't prompted by anything – it just happens. Pathological laughter has nothing to do with feeling happy or sad or any other emotion. It's a disorder in one's emotional expression, and it's often treated with prescription antidepressants.

For anyone who bursts out in unexplained and uncontrollable laughter, the first step should be an appointment with a neurologist. Some researchers feel that uncontrollable and prolonged fits of laughter may be a sign of brain damage caused by disease or injury. If certain neural pathways are interrupted, the brain doesn't receive the information it needs to control laughter or crying.

Along with uncontrollable laughter, the patient may experience uncontrollable body movements or a disturbed mental state. Some with this condition find the laugh attacks pleasant. Others feel nothing positive while they're happening. To others this laughter often appears unnatural and forced. But sometimes it feels so real that it becomes contagious. In such cases, people don't even realize that the laughter is caused by a neurological condition.

Pathological laughing can indicate dangerous issues, such as a stroke in the brain stem or the presence of a brain tumour. Doctors have also noted PLC in people who have Parkinson's disease, multiple sclerosis or types of dementia. Another cause is a condition known as pseudobulbar palsy syndrome. People with this medical issue have difficulty controlling their facial movements, including jaw, tongue and throat muscles. This neurological disorder can make eating, swallowing and speaking difficult.

Laughing is powerful, and that isn't always a great thing for everyone.

So far there is no cure for pseudobulbar palsy syndrome. Doctors may use medication or other treatments to manage the symptoms. But one of the best ways to help is to be aware of the condition and understand it. Often, if those who suffer from this syndrome know their loved ones are there for them and understand their situation, their stress is greatly reduced. Their symptoms may even lessen and the condition improve. That is to say, *not* laughing about it is part of the solution.

Laughing is powerful, and that isn't always a great thing for everyone. Anyone who has been the target of mocking laughter could tell you that. The next time you get the impulse to laugh *at* someone rather than *with* them, think twice. Don't be a *katagelastic* – the scientific term for someone who enjoys laughing at other people. You don't know what damage you may be doing.

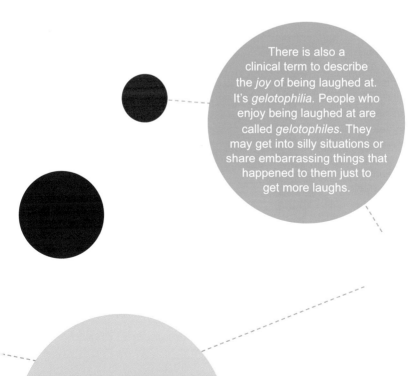

There is also a clinical term to describe the *joy* of being laughed at. It's *gelotophilia*. People who enjoy being laughed at are called *gelotophiles*. They may get into silly situations or share embarrassing things that happened to them just to get more laughs.

CHAPTER 6

The hopefulness of humour

HOW OFTEN DO YOU LAUGH every day? On how many days of the year do you have a good, gut-busting guffaw? Did you know that the more you laugh, the better off you are? Laughing out loud can do wonders for you in more ways than you might imagine.

Imagine that you're part of an audience waiting for a speaker who's about to give a presentation. The mood in the crowd might be expectation or excitement. It may be nervousness, depending on the topic. It might even be boredom. But then the speaker takes the microphone, and the first words out of her mouth are something funny. Laughter ripples through the audience. What has the speaker just done?

She's created a bonding effect. She's made you like her – or at least made you more open to what she'll say next. Most of all, she's relieved the tension of the waiting phase. This is a good example of laughter being the best medicine. We're ready to rock with the presentation, we're emotionally open. Our mental stress might have gone down a notch.

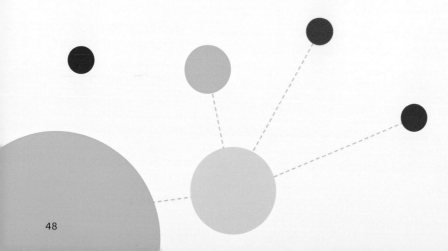

Laughter offers big benefits to your body as well. Consider your heart. That big muscle keeps on keeping on, day and night. And with every big belly laugh, you give that very vital organ an excellent added workout. In fact, the list of physiological benefits you get from laughing goes on and on. That's the hopefulness of humour. It's amazing what a few chuckles can do!

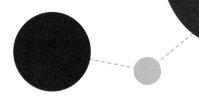

What's your game?

Neurochemical name	Neurochemical game
dopamine	Some people call dopamine the "happiness drug". It motivates people to accomplish tasks or goals, and it rewards them with feelings of satisfaction when those goals are achieved.
oxytocin	You're feeling all warm and cosy about someone. Your heart flutters. You have a moving moment of empathy or of close connection to somebody else. In these cases, oxytocin is doing its thing. It plays a big part in making us the social creatures we are.
serotonin	Life is good. You've never felt better. You're so relaxed that laughing comes easily. If that's how you feel, serotonin is no doubt flowing freely through your system. This neurochemical is often released when you've achieved something significant or important. It plays a big role in regulating sleep, moods, memory and more.
endorphins	If you need to power through something, you've got a stream of endorphins acting on your behalf. This little neurochemical helps you get through times of pain or stress. It dampens down any discomfort you might be feeling. For instance, you know how good you feel after an intense workout? That's your endorphins at work. And hearty laughter is excellent exercise, working out your stomach muscles and a lot more. The more you laugh, the greater your endorphin reward.

JUST THINK ABOUT IT

In a small study, 16 volunteers were divided into two groups. One group was told they were about to watch a funny video, but the other participants didn't get this information. Then the researchers took blood samples from each group. The blood of people who thought they were about to watch something funny showed 87 per cent more human growth hormone and 27 per cent more beta-endorphins, a feel-good chemical, than the people who didn't know what was coming. During the video viewing there was an increase in these positive-mood chemicals, and they remained in the blood for 12 to 14 hours afterwards. So, even the anticipating of something funny coming your way is a plus for your body.

It all goes back to the brain. It's the storehouse of your body's neurochemicals, four of which are directly hooked into happiness. Think of them as DOSE: dopamine, oxytocin, serotonin and endorphins. Different experiences release these chemicals and naturally improve your mood. Endorphins, the body's painkillers, have a close connection to laughter. Every time something tickles your funny bone and you laugh, you set the endorphins free. And that's what makes healthy laughter feel so good.

Studies have shown that just 20 seconds of laughter can benefit your lungs more than three minutes on a rowing machine.

THE BENEFITS OF A BIG LAUGH

- Improves communication and co-operation
- In stressful situations, creates psychological distance so you feel safer
- Oxygenates the blood with every breath, flushing the lymphatic system and eliminating toxins 15 times more quickly than normal breathing does
- Powers up the immune system
- Increases bloodstream content of immunoglobulin A, an antibody that attacks viral and bacterial infections in the intestinal and upper respiratory tracts
- Stimulates circulation, thus reducing muscle tension, which leads to greater relaxation
- Reduces the flow of stress hormones such as serum cortisol, adrenaline and epinephrine
- Decreases the possibility of future stroke and cardiovascular disease as well as other health issues related to stress
- May decrease blood sugar levels

Word to the wise: Don't hold back your hilarity, even if you feel your laugh is too loud or otherwise odd. You'll live happier and healthier with lots of laughter!

LAUGH YOURSELF SILLY

Why not instigate a little wild laughter among your friends? Do it this way: Lie down on the floor with each person's head resting on another person's stomach. The first person says, "Ha!" The person whose head is on that person's stomach says, "Ha ha!" And so on. It probably won't be long before you're all wailing with laughter. How many does it take to make a laugh-in? The more the merrier!

Think of the last time you laughed out loud at a funny film. That was a guaranteed boost to your immunity. Researchers at Indiana State University in the USA asked one group of volunteers to sit through a laugh-inducing comedy while another group was stuck with a dull travel video. Afterwards, the scientists studied immune cells from the participants in each group. The group that had laughed out loud had higher numbers of immune cells than the group that yawned through their film. It seems that, in most cases, the more you laugh, the more disease-resistant you become.

Getting caught up in a good case of the giggles is like a bonus prize for your whole being. Laughter truly is great medicine for all of us!

Benefits of laughter

Strengthens your memory

Releases endorphins and puts you in a good mood

Increases your creativity and problem-solving skills

Lessens muscle tension

Helps with depression and anxiety

Improves blood flow in body

Increases pain tolerance

Benjamin Franklin

THE SIGNIFICANCE OF SATIRE

It's been around since at least ancient Greece. Author, inventor and politician Benjamin Franklin showed his talent for it in the 1700s. A century later another American author, Mark Twain, became known as a master of the same. We're talking about satire, a type of humour that gets people laughing by poking fun at the systems and process that underlie society, government, fashion trends, the rich and powerful and much more.

Throughout history, writing or speaking out in a satirical way has often been a risky business. That's because satire usually challenges authority in one form or another. While they're laughing, people sit up and take notice of things they might not have been aware of or that they were worried about mentioning themselves.

That's why comedians such as Ricky Gervais and Sarah Millican have been so successful on TV in recent years. Like some ancient Greek playwrights, they call out society's shortcomings and hypocrisy. And they do it in such a witty way that you can't help laughing. The same is true of parody, satire's closely related cousin. Parody is the art of imitating something or someone real while putting a humorous spin on it.

Both satire and parody are important forms of social comedy, and not just because you get a good laugh. Some scientists have found that these types of humour are motivating young people to do more than watch and giggle. Children laugh at what they hear or see – and then they go out and learn more about the topics the comics addressed.

Eleven tips for laughing more

US author Mark Twain said, "Humour is the great thing, the saving thing . . . The minute it crops up, all our hardnesses yield, all our irritations and resentments flit away, and a sunny spirit takes their place." Try these suggestions to cultivate that "sunny spirit" and bring more laughter into your life.

Play fun, competitive party-type games with your friends.

Hang out as much as possible with the funniest people you can find.

Make a list of funny films and sitcoms and watch them as often as you can.

Laughing inspiration

Listen to funny podcasts.

Read a funny book or comic.

Babysit or just spend time with a child – ask deep questions and enjoy their funny answers.

Spend less time with those who are humourless.

Remember favourite funny moments with people who were there with you at the time.

Watch funny YouTube videos. Search "funniest teen fails" or watch cat videos and clips of babies laughing.

Look for humour wherever you go. If you're consciously looking for it, you'll find it!

Don't forget to find ways to laugh at yourself once in a while.

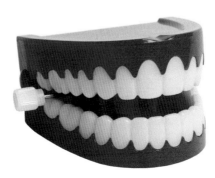

Reach out

Statistics show that many children today struggle with depression and anxiety. One of the best ways to remedy a serious down-in-the-dumps slump is something that's trending strongly in many parts of the world: laughter yoga.

The idea of joining a laughter yoga group might seem silly at first. However, if you'd like some fun, this might be for you even if you're not into twisting your body into pretzel positions. It combines laughter with the deep-breathing exercises of physical yoga and a bit of mindfulness meditation to bring a feeling of happiness. These groups aim to incorporate what some laughter yoga teachers call "the four elements of joy" – laughter, dancing, singing and play – into the exercises. This gives you an experience that's both calming and invigorating. No matter what mood you're in when you walk into a laughter yoga session, you'll walk out feeling refreshed and upbeat.

Laughter yoga was created by Dr Madan Kataria in Mumbai, India, in the 1990s, and it's been steadily gaining popularity. Laughter yoga teachers cite many benefits in starting young. These techniques are good at reducing stress and anxiety. Laughter yoga can also increase your joyfulness, foster self-confidence, give you more mental focus, and just help you deal with everyday life.

Laughter yoga is becoming increasingly popular. According to some reports, more than 5,000 laughter yoga clubs now exist in more than 50 countries. Why not think about starting one at your school?

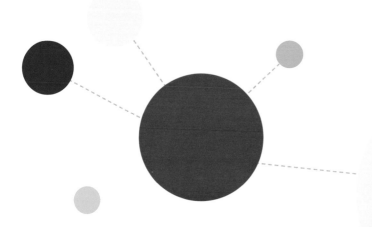

Glossary

affect set of physical reactions to an experienced emotion

anthropomorphic giving human qualities to non-human creatures or objects

demeaned lowered in status or reputation

dominance having a position of power or control, especially in a group

epidemic something that occurs in a widespread way, usually negative

gelotology study of laughter

incongruity theory theory that humour arises when a familiar pattern is broken by something illogical or unfamiliar

inferiority condition of being lower in quality, accomplishment or status

irony using words in a way that expresses something other than, or even exactly opposite to, their literal meaning

larynx hollow voice box in the throat that delivers air to the lungs and contains the vocal cords

limbic system structures and areas of the nervous system that are associated with emotions, instincts and memory

neurologist medical doctor who specializes in the functions and problems of the nerves and nervous system

ostracized left out or excluded from a group

pathological indicating or caused by a diseased or disordered condition; extreme in an abnormal way

radioactive releasing energetic particles

relief theory theory that humour arises to relieve tension

sophisticated at a higher or more intellectual level

superiority theory theory, first suggested by Plato, that humour arises when laughers feel as if they are better than the person they're laughing at

Find out more

Books

Brain Games: The Mind-Blowing Science of Your Amazing Brain, Jennifer Swanson, (National Geographic Kids, 2016)

Laugh-Out-Loud Jokes to Tell Your Friends, (Jokes, Tricks and Other Funny Stuff), Michael Dahl, (Raintree, 2018)

The Art of Being a Brilliant Teenager, Andy Cope, (Capstone, 2015)

Your Brain and Body (Your Mind Matters), Honor Head, (Hodder Education, 2017)

Websites

science.howstuffworks.com/life/inside-the-mind/emotions/laughter.htm
More scientific detail about how the brain affects laughter, where laughter comes from and the purpose of laughter, including facts, video clips and interactive diagrams.

www.mind.org.uk
Information for children, teenagers and parents about mental health and wellbeing and how to find support.

www.youngminds.org.uk/find-help/looking-after-yourself/take-time-out/
Strategies to encourage a positive mindset and lots of tips to help you develop stress-busting techniques.

Comprehension questions

1

What circumstances can you think of in which laughter might have helped people survive?

2

What are some different reasons for inappropriate or uncontrollable laughter? Contrast the ways in which such laughter can be either positive or negative. If you have ever experienced inappropriate laughter, what brought it on?

3

Different cultures do not always find humour in the same things. What might be some reasons for this? How would you react if someone from another culture laughed at something you didn't think was appropriate to laugh about?

4

What is the difference between laughter and speech when it comes to brain functioning?

Source notes

p. 4, "People throughout history have laughed . . ." Robert Provine, "Why We Laugh," *The Atlantic,* Atlantic Documentaries, June 5, 2014, 0:25 seconds, https:// www.theatlantic.com/video/index/372213/why-we-laugh/ Accessed March 7, 2019.

p. 11, "The caretakers play with the apes. . ." Ian Sample, "Our Primate Ancestors Have Been Laughing for 10m Years," *The Guardian,* June 4, 2009, https://www .theguardian.com/science/2009/jun/04/laughter-primates-apes-evolution-tickling Accessed March 7, 2019.

p. 25, "Plato and Aristotle . . ." Robert Provine, "Why We Laugh," 4:45, https:// www.theatlantic.com/video/index/372213/why-we-laugh/ Accessed March 7, 2019.

p. 28, "laughter does in the nervous system . . ." John Morreall, "Philosophy of Humor," *Stanford Encyclopedia of Philosophy,* September 28, 2016, https://plato .stanford.edu/entries/humor/ Accessed March 7, 2019.

p. 35, "When we laugh . . ." Antoinette May, interview with Annette Goodheart, *Science of the Mind* (September 1988), quoted in Sebastian Gendry, "How Annette Goodheart Did It," https://www.laughteronlineuniversity.com/laughter-therapy -annette-goodheart/ Accessed March 7, 2019.

p. 36, "our own body makes us start laughing. . ." Rebecca Kamm, "Experts Explain Why You Laugh When You Shouldn't," Vice, January 19, 2018, https://www.vice .com/en_uk/article/yw55yw/experts-explain-why-you-laugh-when-you-shouldnt Accessed March 7, 2019.

p. 40, "In our feel-good . . ." Robert Provine, "Why We Laugh," 4:32, https://www .theatlantic.com/video/index/372213/why-we-laugh/ Accessed March 7, 2019.

p. 43, "Many people who are teased . . ." Antoinette May, interview with Annette Goodheart, *Science of the Mind* (September 1988), quoted in Sebastian Gendry, "How Annette Goodheart Did It," https://www.laughteronlineuniversity.com/laughter -therapy-annette-goodheart/ Accessed March 7, 2019.

p. 56, "Humor is the great thing . . ." Mark Twain, "What Paul Bourget Thinks of Us," *How to Tell a Story and Other Essays.* New York: American Publishing, 1909, p. 163.

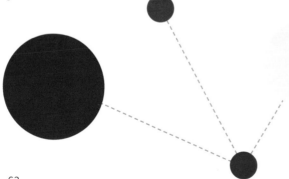

Select bibliography

Brain, Marshall, "How Laughter Works," How Stuff Works, https://science.howstuffworks.com/life/inside-the-mind/emotions/laughter2.htm Accessed March 7, 2019.

Cao, Stella, "Laughter Across the Animal Kingdom, from Rats to Humans," Yale Scientific, November 4, 2012, http://www.yalescientific.org/2012/11/laughter-across-the-animal-kingdom-from-rats-to-humans/ Accessed March 7, 2019.

Kamm, Rebecca, "Experts Explain Why You Laugh When You Shouldn't," Vice, January 19, 2018, https://www.vice.com/en_uk/article/yw55yw/experts-explain-why-you-laugh-when-you-shouldnt Accessed March 7, 2019.

Langer, Emily, "Jaak Panksepp, 'Rat Tickler' Who Revealed Emotional Lives of Animals, Dies at 73," *Washington Post,* April 21, 2017, https://www.washingtonpost.com/national/health-science/jaak-panksepp-rat-tickler-who-revealed-emotional-lives-of-animals-dies-at-73/2017/04/21/01e367ce-2536-11e7-a1b3-faff0034e2de_story.html Accessed March 7, 2019.

May, Antoinette, interview with Annette Goodheart, *Science of the Mind* (September 1988), quoted in Sebastian Gendry, "How Annette Goodheart Did It," https://www.laughteronlineuniversity.com/laughter-therapy-annette-goodheart/ Accessed March 7, 2019.

Morreall, John, "Philosophy of Humor," Stanford Encyclopedia of Philosophy, September 28, 2016, https://plato.stanford.edu/entries/humor/ Accessed March 7, 2019.

Provine, Robert R., "The Science of Laughter," Psychology Today, November 1, 2000, https://www.psychologytoday.com/us/articles/200011/the-science-laughter Accessed March 7, 2019.

———, "Why We Laugh," *The Atlantic,* Atlantic Documentaries, June 5, 2014, https://www.theatlantic.com/video/index/372213/why-we-laugh/ Accessed March 7, 2019.

Sample, Ian, "Our Primate Ancestors Have Been Laughing for 10m Years," *The Guardian,* June 4, 2009, https://www.theguardian.com/science/2009/jun/04/laughter-primates-apes-evolution-tickling Accessed March 7, 2019.

Scott, Sophie, "10 Things You May Not Know About Laughter," BBC, October 26, 2014, https://www.bbc.com/news/health-29754636 Accessed March 7, 2019.

———, "The Science of Laughter," BBC, September 11, 2016, https://www.bbc.com/news/health-37311320 Accessed March 7, 2019.

Stephens, Pippa, "Gelotophobia: Living a Life in Fear of Laughter," BBC, June 27, 2014, https://www.bbc.com/news/health-27323470 Accessed March 7, 2019.

Thompson, Andrea, "Study: Laughter Really Is Contagious," Live Science, December 12, 2006, https://www.livescience.com/6946-joke-animals-laugh.html Accessed March 7, 2019.

Twain, Mark. *How to Tell a Story and Other Essays.* New York: American Publishing, 1909.

Index

About the author

Pamela Dell was born in Idaho, grew up in Chicago, and has lived most of her adult life in Los Angeles and San Francisco (all in the USA) where she created an award-winning series of computer games for girls. Today, Pamela divides her time between Chicago and California in the USA, writing and editing books for young people. She has published more than 80 children's books, both fiction and non-fiction.